J 3-4 811.54 GERATY
Geraty, Virginia Mixson.
Gullah night before
Christmas / by Virginia M.
Geraty ; illustrated by
James Rice.

Gullah Night Before Christmas

Gullah Night Before Christmas

By Virginia M. Geraty
Illustrated by James Rice

PELICAN PUBLISHING COMPANY
Gretna 1998

For Luke, Anna, Sara, and Bradford

*The word "Pelican" and the depiction of a pelican are trademarks
of Pelican Publishing Company, Inc., and are registered
in the U.S. Patent and Trademark Office.*

Library of Congress Cataloging-in-Publication Data

Geraty, Viginia Mixson.
    Gullah night before Christmas / by Virginia M. Geraty ;
illustrated by James Rice.
        p.   cm.
    Summary: A version, told in the Gullah dialect, of the
familiar poem about the annual Christmas visit of Santa
Claus in which "Sandy Claw" is represented by "Buh Rabbit."
    ISBN 1-56554-330-0 (hardcover : alk. paper)
    1. Sea Islands Creole dialect—Texts. 2. Santa Claus—
Juvenile poetry. 3. Christmas—Juvenile poetry. [1. Santa
Claus—Poetry. 2. Christmas—Poetry. 3. Gullahs—Poetry. 4.
Narrative poetry. 5. American poetry. 6. Sea Islands Creole
dialect.] I. Rice, James, 1934- ill. II. Title.
PM7875.G8G468 1998
427'.975799—dc21   97-40690
                                                         CIP
                                                          AC

Printed in Hong Kong

Published by Pelican Publishing Company, Inc.
P.O. Box 3110, Gretna, Louisiana 70054-3110

Gullah Night Before Christmas

'E bin de night befo' Chris'mus en' eenside we house,
Eb'ryt'ing settle down, eb'n de mouse.
De cump'ny done lef' f'um de bighouse at las',
En' de fambly all gone tuh Middlenight Mass.

W'en all ub uh sudd'n, wuh dat Uh yeddy[1]?
Cyan' be Sandy Claw done git yuh awready!
Fuh true, dey ent bin no rain-deah hoof
Duh prance en' paw 'puntop'uh de roof!

1. yeddy—hear, heard

Ef dis bin uh haant cum'fuh mek fun,
Uh gwi' kill'um 'gen 'fo' 'e kin run.

Uh graff up de fiah-pokuh en' op'n de do'.
Uh sway' Uh nebbuh bin so 'sprize befo'.

Dey "Sandy Claw Buh Rabbit" wid uh gunnysack
Full wid Chris'mus gif' flung 'cross 'e back!

'E say Merry Chris'mus en' 'e haffuh mek'ace
'Kase Buh Fox on 'e tail, en' 'e done g'em chase!

'E fuhr bin all tangledy wid briah en' du't,
En' 'e run all de way bidout uh shoesh tuh 'e foot.
'E yez binnuh droop, 'e yeye[2] still yet twinkledy.
Uh haffuh laff w'en Uh shum[3], 'e nose bin so wrinkledy.

2. yeye—eyes
3. shum—saw him

Uh holluh tuh Mamma, "Us ent haffuh worry!
Dis Sandy Claw, yuh! 'E sawtuh een uh hurry."
Uh ax Sandy huccome de rain-deah ent pass.
'E say 'e lef'um home; 'e own foot mo' fas'.

'E say 'e haffuh dus' 'roun' en' done 'fo' dayclean[4]
'Kase Buh Fox right behin'um en' Buh Fox dat mean—
'E gwi' t'row'um een de briah-patch, en t'ief de present too,
Ef him kin obuhreach'um 'fo' 'e gitt'ru!

4. 'fo' dayclean—before daylight

Uh tell Sandy Rabbit mus'
set en' res' 'e feet,
   W'ile Uh gone tuh de
kitchun fuh sump'n fuhr'um
eat.
   Sandy say t'engky en 'e
haffuh nyam'um[5] quick,
   'Fo' Buh Fox git yuh en'
nyam Ole Saint Nick.

5. nyam'um—eat it

So, Uh fetch'um some collud green, some hom'ny en' ham,
Some hoecake en' syrup fuh Sandy Claw nyam.

Sandy nyam de bittle en' gone skrate tuh 'e wu'k.
'E full all de sox, den 'e tu'n wid uh ju'k.

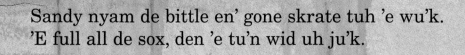

Wid 'e lef' han' paw, 'e wipe 'e nose.
'E say, "Merry Chris'mus," en' out 'e goes!
Uh watch'um 'tell 'e mos' gone out me sight
'En pray Buh Fox ent ketch'um dis night.

Uh lock up good-fashi'n, en' w'en Uh tu'n 'roun',
Down de chimbly come Buh Fox—de 'ceitful ole houn'!
'E fuhr ent git swinge, same luk 'e oughtuh,
'Kase 'e wet 'e se'f down wid us rain-barril watuh!

'E cuss, "Drat dat rabbit! Uh figguh fuh sho'
Uh gwi' ketch'um dis time 'fo' 'e git out de do'."
Uh know ole Buh Fox uh berry soon-man[6]
En' Uh gwi' try fuh hol'um long ez Uh can,

Fuh gib Sandy time fuh gone on 'e way—
So de chillun hab present come Chris'mus Day.
Uh gone tell Mamma mus' come'yuh quick
En' talk tuh Buh Fox w'ile Uh gone fuh waa'n Saint Nick!

6. berry soon-man—a smart man

Uh lickedy-split down de road so fas'
Uh git tuh de nex' house 'fo' uh minit done pass.

Uh bus’ op’n de do’ en’ holluh tuh Sandy,
“Buh Fox tuh we house duh nyam all de candy!

“Mamma gwi’ hol’um long ez ’e kin,
’Cep’ you know ole Buh Fox tricky ez sin.”
Sandy Claw Buh Rabbit tek ’e foot een ’e han’
En’ tell you dat crittuh bin uh fas’ leetle man!

Uh gone back tuh we house, figguh Buh Fox done 'scape.
'E dey duh tell Mamma 'bout de sour grape.
'E say 'e gwine now 'kase 'e haffuh dus' 'roun'
Fuh ketch Buh Rabbit 'fo' 'e git tuh de town!

'E mek 'e mannus, dat sly ole dandy.

Den 'e graff de apple, de sky-rocket, en' de candy.

'E jump up een de chimbly, de fiah bu'n down low,
'Cep' 'e foot slip een 'e hurry, en' 'e fall back on de flo'.

De chillun apple wuh 'e done try fuh take
Drap down on de haa'th en' den staa't fuh bake.
'E jump up 'gen en' try fuh rise,
Dat w'en us hab uh big 'sprize.

De skyrocket lan' on de red-hot embuh
En' blas' Buh Fox clean out ub Decembuh!
Uh gone tuh de do' quick ez uh flash,
Uh figguh fuh true 'e gwi' lan' wid uh crash.

'Cep' Uh shum clim' mo' highuh en' highuh,
Same likkuh comet, wid 'e tail on fiah.
Den w'en 'e git way up een de sky,
'E holluh, "Chris'mus gif"[7], Lawd, 'kase Uh
comin' by!"

7. "Chris'mus gif'"—This is an old Christmas custom. When two people greet on Christmas Day, the first one to say "Christmas gift" receives a gift from the other.

De chillun laff fuh tru, w'en dey yeddy 'bout de ruckus
En' all ub we hab bake apple fuh brukwus.
Nutt'n ent dey dey een de chillun sox,
Stillyet dey say uh pray fuh po' ole Buh Fox.

Glossary

bighouse—the plantation owner's house
Middlenight Mass—Mass at midnight on Christmas Eve
yeddy—hear, heard
rain-deah—reindeer
haant—ghost
mek fun—play a joke
graff—grabbed
fiah-pokuh—fire poker
sway'—swear
haffuh mek'ace—has to hurry
g'em chase—tried to catch him
fuhr—fur
bidout—without
yez—ears
yeye—eyes
shum—saw him
sawtuh—sort of
huccome—how come, why
dus' 'roun'—move hurriedly
'fo' dayclean—before daylight
obuhreach'um—catch him
nyam'um—eat it
bittle—victuals, food
good-fashi'n—well
swinge—singed
berry soon-man—a smart man
waa'n—warn
'cep'—except
tek 'e foot een 'e han'—to take his foot in his hand; to hurry
mek 'e mannus—said good-bye politely
haa'th—hearth
"Chris'mus gif'"—This is an old Christmas custom. When two
    people greet on Christmas Day, the first one to say "Christmas
    gift" receives a gift from the other.
nutt'n ent dey dey—nothing is there
stillyet—still